TO



Mahima

FROM

Amma

DATE

11/7/11

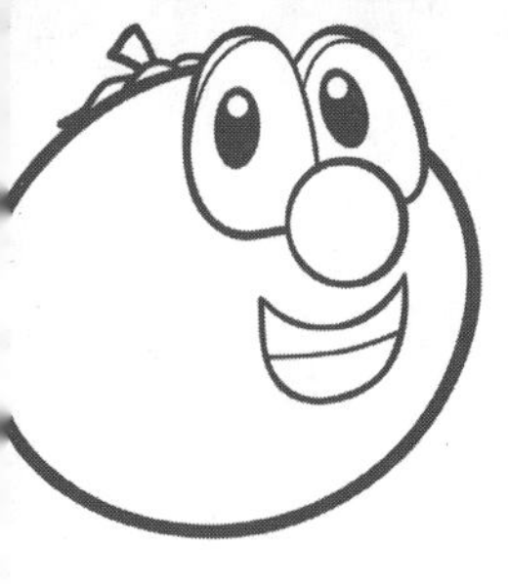

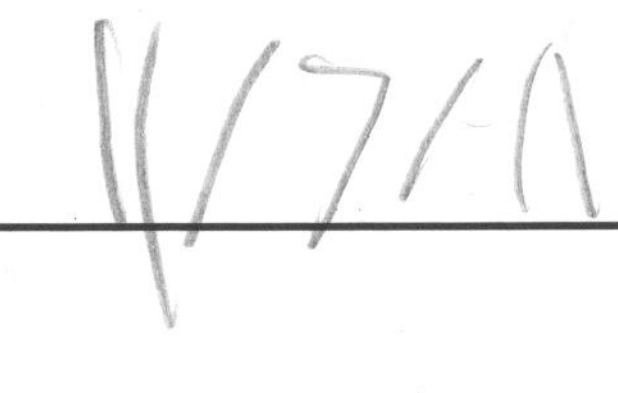

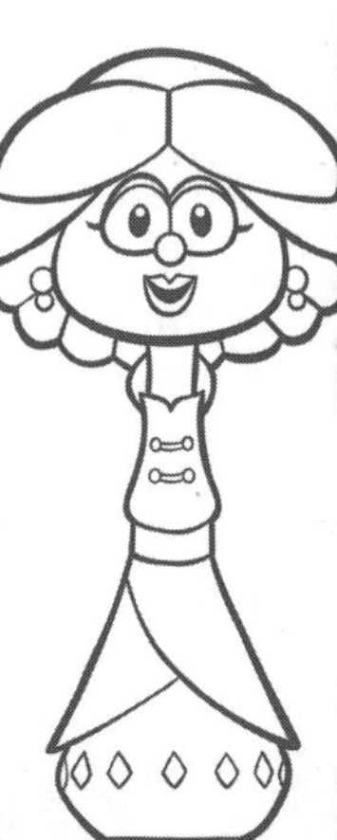

BIG IDEA
bigidea.com

VeggieTales®

# 30 Very Veggie Devos about Kindness

*The quoted ideas expressed in this book (but not scripture verses) are not, in all cases, exact quotations, as some have been edited for clarity and brevity. In all cases, the author has attempted to maintain the speaker's original intent. In some cases, quoted material for this book was obtained from secondary sources, primarily print media. While every effort was made to ensure the accuracy of these sources, the accuracy cannot be guaranteed. For additions, deletions, corrections or clarifications in future editions of this text, please write* BIG IDEA©.



Cover Design by Big Idea Design
Page Layout by Bart Dawson

ISBN 978-160587-131-8

*Printed in the United States of America*

VeggieTales®

# 30 Very Veggie Devos About Kindness

# TABLE OF CONTENTS

# A MESSAGE FOR PARENTS

If you're already familiar with VeggieTales®, you know the importance of providing your youngster with a steady stream of big ideas from God's Word. And this VeggieTales® devotional book can help you do just that.

This little text contains 30 brief chapters, one for each day of the month. Each chapter consists of a Bible verse, a brief story or lesson, kid-friendly quotations from notable Christian thinkers, a timely tip, and a prayer. Every chapter examines a different aspect of an important Biblical theme: kindness.

So please try this experiment: For the next 30 days, take the time to read one chapter each night to your child, and then spend a few moments talking about the chapter's meaning. By the end of the month, you will have had 30 different opportunities to share God's wisdom with your son or daughter, and that's good . . . very good.

If you have been touched by God's love and His grace, then you know the joy that He has brought into your own life. Now it's your turn to share His message with the boy or girl whom He has entrusted to your care. Happy reading! And may God richly bless you and your family now and forever.

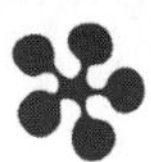
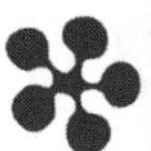

# A MESSAGE TO KIDS

Have you seen the VeggieTales® episode called *Tomato Sawyer and Huckleberry Larry's Big River Rescue?* If so, you probably remember Bob and Larry took lots of chances to help a mysterious singing stranger. And by the end of the adventure, Bob and Larry figured out an important lesson. They learned that God wants all of us to help each other whenever we can. That's why the big ideas in this book—ideas about what it means to be helpful and kind—are really important.

So for the next month, ask your mom or dad to help you read a chapter a day. When you do, you'll be reminded that it's nice to be important, but it's more important to be nice.

Always try to do
what is good for each other
and for all people.

1 Thessalonians 5:15 ICB

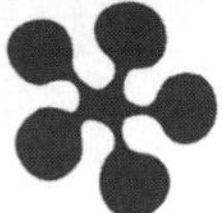

# KINDNESS STARTS WITH YOU!

We must not become tired of doing good.
We will receive our harvest of eternal life
at the right time. We must not give up!

Galatians 6:9 ICB

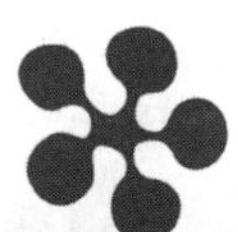

If you're waiting for other people to be nice to you before you're nice to them, you've got it backwards. Kindness starts with you! You see, you can never control what other people will say or do, but you can control your own behavior.

The Bible tells us that we should never stop doing good deeds as long as we live. Kindness is God's way, and it should be our way, too. Starting now!

We ought not to be weary of doing little things for the love of God, who regards not the greatness of the work, but the love with which it is performed.

Brother Lawrence

Faith never asks whether good works are to be done, but has done them before there is time to ask the question, and it is always doing them.

Martin Luther

## TODAY'S BRIGHT IDEA

Kindness every day: Kindness should be part of our lives every day, not just on the days when we feel good. Don't try to be kind some of the time, and don't try to be kind to some of the people you know. Instead, try to be kind all of the time, and try to be kind to all of the people you know.

## PRAYER OF THE DAY

Dear Lord, help me to remember
that it is always my job to treat others
with kindness and respect.
Make the Golden Rule my rule
and make Your Word my guidebook
for the way I treat other people.
Amen

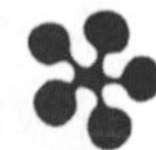

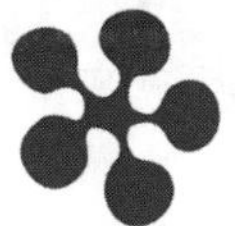

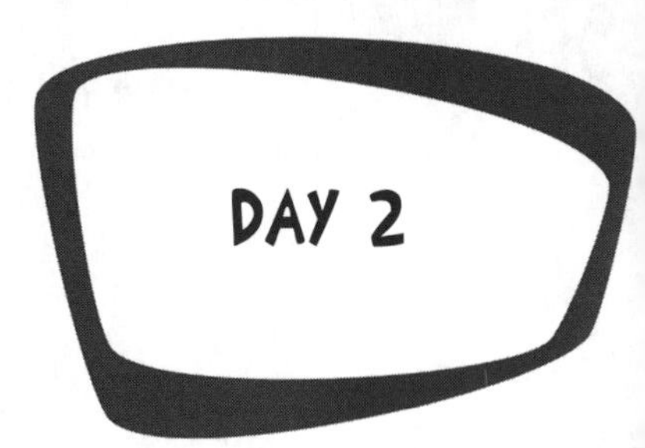

## DAY 2

# HIS NAME WAS BARNABAS

Barnabas was a good man,
full of the Holy Spirit and full of faith.

Acts 11:23-24 ICB

Barnabas was a leader in the early Christian church who was known for his kindness and for his ability to encourage others. Because of Barnabas, many people were introduced to Christ.

We become like Barnabas when we speak kind words to our families and to our friends. And then, because we have been generous and kind, the people around us can see how Christians should behave. So when in doubt, be kind and generous to others, just like Barnabas.

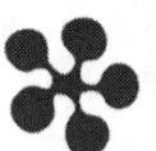

We can't all be heroes because somebody has to sit on the curb and applaud when they go by.

Will Rogers

When someone does something good, applaud! You'll make two people feel good.

Sam Goldwyn

## TODAY'S BRIGHT IDEA

Be an encourager! Barnabas was known as a man who encouraged others. In other words, he made other people feel better by saying kind things. You, like Barnabas, can encourage your family and friends . . . and you should.

## PRAYER OF THE DAY

Dear Lord, let me help to encourage other people by the words that I say and the things that I do. Let me be a person who is always helpful and kind to my friends and family. And let them see Your love for me reflected in my love for them.

Amen

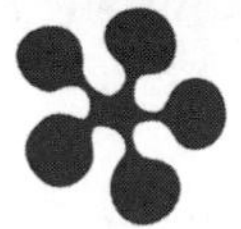

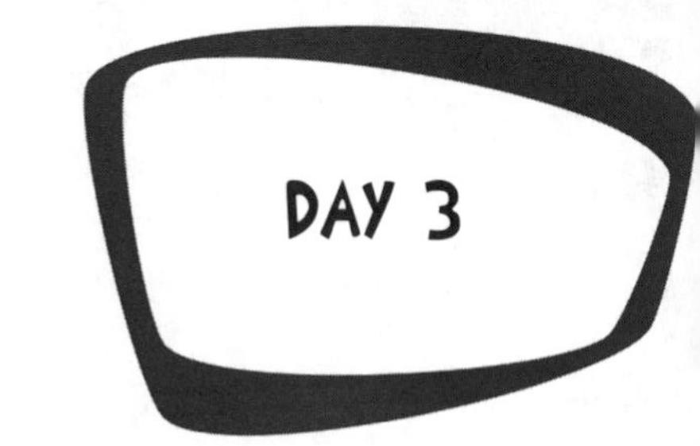


# DON'T BE CRUEL!

Don't ever stop being kind and truthful.
Let kindness and truth show in all you do.

Proverbs 3:3 ICB

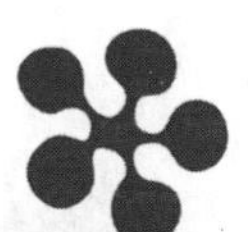

Sometimes, young people can be very mean. They can make fun of other people, and when they do so, it's wrong. Period.

As Christians, we should be kind to everyone. And, if other kids say unkind things to a child or make fun of him or her, it's up to us to step in, like the Good Samaritan, and lend a helping hand.

Today and every day, be a person who is known for your kindness, not for your cruelty. That's how God wants you to behave. Period.

There's a lot in the world we ought to be very angry about: oppression, injustice, discrimination, and cruelty that mistreats the poor and makes fun of the disabled.

Bill Hybels

Discouraged people don't need critics. They hurt enough already. They don't need more guilt or piled-on distress. They need encouragement. They need a refuge, a willing, caring, available someone.

Charles Swindoll

## TODAY'S BRIGHT IDEA

Stand up and be counted! Do you know children who say or do cruel things to other kids? If so, don't join in! Instead, stand up for those who need your help. It's the right thing to do.

## PRAYER OF THE DAY

Dear Lord, when I see meanness in this
world, let me do my best to correct it.
When I see people who are hurting,
let me do my best to help them.
And when I am hurt by others,
let me do my best to forgive them.
Amen

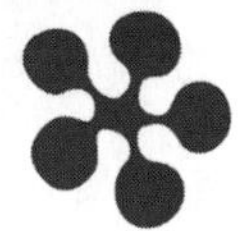

# THE THINGS WE SAY

A good person's words will help many others.

Proverbs 10:21 ICB

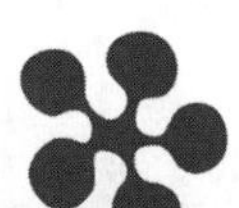

The words that we speak are very important because of how they effect other people. The things that we say can either help people or hurt them. We can either make people feel better, or we can hurt their feelings.

The Bible reminds us that words are powerful things; we must use them carefully. Let's use our words to help our families and friends. When we do, we make their lives better and our own.

We do have the ability to encourage or discourage each other with the words we say. In order to maintain a positive mood, our hearts must be in good condition.

Annie Chapman

So often we think that to be encouragers we have to produce great words of wisdom when, in fact, a few simple syllables of sympathy and an arm around the shoulder can often provide much needed comfort.

Florence Littauer

## TODAY'S BRIGHT IDEA

Think first, speak second: If you want to keep from hurting other people's feelings, don't open your mouth until you've turned on your brain.

## PRAYER OF THE DAY

Dear Lord, make my words pleasing to You. Let the words that I say and the things that I do help others to feel better about themselves and to know more about You.
Amen

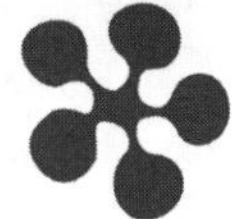

# THE RULE THAT'S GOLDEN

Do for other people the same things
you want them to do for you.

Matthew 7:12 ICB

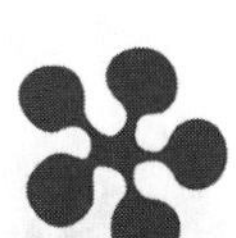

Some rules are easier to understand than they are to live by. Jesus told us that we should treat other people in the same way that we would want to be treated: that's the Golden Rule. But sometimes, especially when we're tired or upset, that rule is very hard to follow.

Jesus wants us to treat other people with respect, love, kindness, and courtesy. When we do, we make our families and friends happy . . . and we make our Father in heaven very proud. So if you're wondering how to treat someone else, ask the person you see every time you look into the mirror. The answer you receive will tell you exactly what to do.

Let no one ever come to you without leaving better and happier. Be the living expression of God's kindness: kindness in your face, kindness in your eyes, kindness in your smile.

Mother Teresa

Make the most of today.
Translate your good intentions
into actual good deeds.

Grenville Kleiser

## TODAY'S BRIGHT IDEA

How would you feel? When you're trying to decide how to treat another person, ask yourself this question: "How would I feel if somebody treated me that way?" Then, treat the other person the way that you would want to be treated.

## PRAYER OF THE DAY

Dear Lord, help me always to do
my very best to treat others
as I wish to be treated.
The Golden Rule is Your rule,
Father; let me also make it mine.
Amen

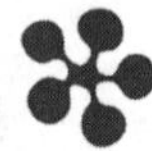

## DAY 6

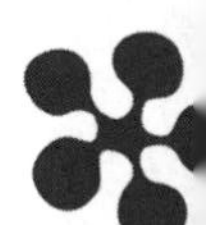

# KIND WORDS

When you talk, do not say harmful things. But say what people need—words that will help them become stronger. Then what you say will help those who listen to you.

Ephesians 4:29 ICB

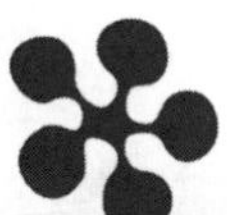

Do you like for people to say kind words to you? Of course you do! And that's exactly how other people feel, too. That's why it's so important to say things that make people feel better, not worse.

Your words can help people . . . or not. Make certain that you're the kind of person who says helpful things, not hurtful things. And, make sure that you're the kind of person who helps other people feel better about themselves, not worse.

Everybody needs to hear kind words, and that's exactly the kind of words they should hear from you!

Words. Do you fully understand their power? Can any of us really grasp the mighty force behind the things we say? Do we stop and think before we speak, considering the potency of the words we utter?

Joni Eareckson Tada

We do have the ability to encourage or discourage each other with the words we say. In order to maintain a positive mood, our hearts must be in good condition.

Annie Chapman

## TODAY'S BRIGHT IDEA

If you can't think of something nice to say . . . don't say anything. It's better to say nothing than to hurt someone's feelings.

# PRAYER OF THE DAY

Dear Lord, You hear every word that I say. Help me remember to speak words that are honest, kind, and helpful.
Amen

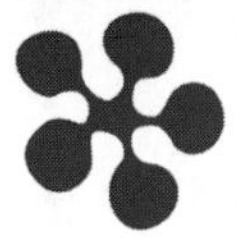

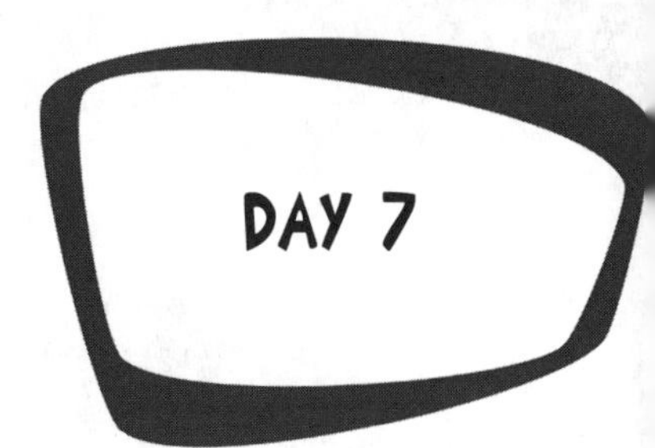

## DAY 7

# HOW WOULD JESUS BEHAVE?

Love other people just as Christ loved us.

Ephesians 5:2 ICB

If you're not sure whether something is right or wrong—kind or unkind—ask yourself a simple question: "How would Jesus behave if He were here?" The answer to that question will tell you what to do.

Jesus was perfect, but we are not. Still, we must try as hard as we can to do the best that we can. When we do, we will love others, just as Christ loves us.

I can tell you, from personal experience of walking with God for over fifty years, that He is the Lover of my soul.

Vonette Bright

A believer comes to Christ; a disciple follows after Him.

Vance Havner

## TODAY'S BRIGHT IDEA

Learning about Jesus: Start learning about Jesus, and keep learning about Him as long as you live. His story never grows old, and His teachings never fail.

## PRAYER OF THE DAY

Dear Lord, let me use Jesus as my guide for living. When I have questions about what to do or how to act, let me behave as He behaved. When I do, I will share His love with my family, with my friends, and with the world.

Amen

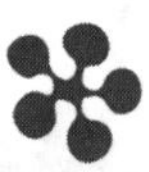

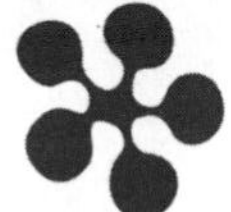

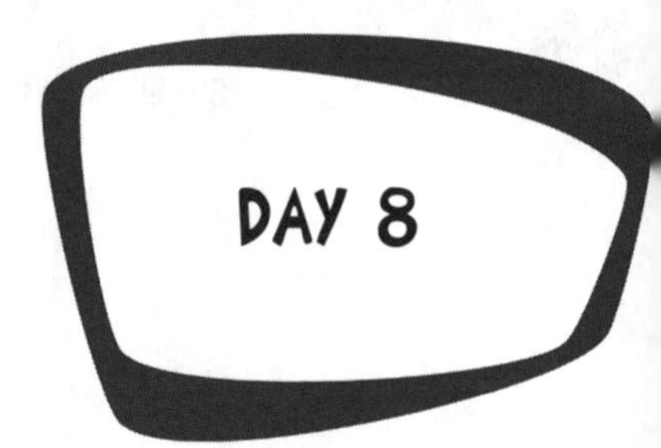

DAY 8

# MAKING OTHER PEOPLE FEEL BETTER!

Let us think about each other
and help each other to show love
and do good deeds.

Hebrews 10:24 ICB

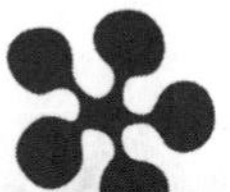

When other people are sad, what can we do? We can do our best to cheer them up by showing kindness and love.

The Bible tells us that we must care for each other, and when everybody is happy, that's an easy thing to do. But, when people are sad, for whatever reason, it's up to us to speak a kind word or to offer a helping hand.

Do you know someone who is discouraged or sad? If so, perhaps it's time to take matters into your own hands. Think of something you can do to cheer that person up . . . and then do it! You'll make two people happy.

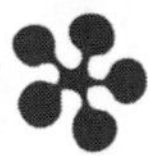

None of us has gotten where we are solely by pulling ourselves up from our own bootstraps. We got here because somebody bent down and helped us.

Thurgood Marshall

What this old world needs is less advice and more helping hands.

Anonymous

## TODAY'S BRIGHT IDEA

Cheering someone up without saying a word: If you want to cheer someone up but can't think of something to say or do, try drawing a picture or writing a note.

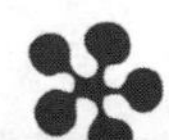

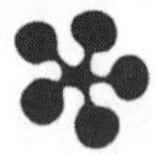

## PRAYER OF THE DAY

Dear Lord, make me a loving,
encouraging Christian.
And, let my love for Jesus be
reflected through the kindness that
I show to those who need the healing
touch of the Master's hand.
Amen

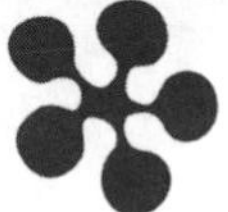

# DO YOURSELF A FAVOR

A kind person is doing himself a favor.
But a cruel person brings
trouble upon himself.

Proverbs 11:17 ICB

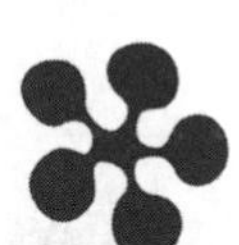

King Solomon wrote most of the Book of Proverbs; in it, he gave us wonderful advice for living wisely. Solomon warned that unkind behavior leads only to trouble, but kindness is its own reward.

The next time you're tempted to say an unkind word, remember Solomon. He was one of the wisest men who ever lived, and he knew that it's always better to be kind. And now, you know it, too.

Kind words do not cost much. Although they cost little, they accomplish much. Kind words produce a beautiful image on men's souls.

Pascal

Always be a little kinder than necessary.

James Barrie

## TODAY'S BRIGHT IDEA

Sorry you said it? Apologize! Did you say something that hurt someone's feelings? Then it's time for an apology: yours. It's never too late to apologize, but it's never too early, either!

## PRAYER OF THE DAY

Dear Lord, let me be a kind person.
Let me be quick to share and quick
to forgive. And when I make mistakes,
let me be quick to change and quick
to ask forgiveness from
others and from You.
Amen

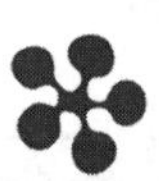

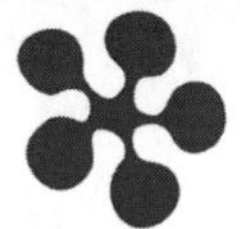

DAY 10

# THE GOOD SAMARITAN

Help each other with your troubles.
When you do this,
you truly obey the law of Christ.

Galatians 6:2 ICB

Jesus told the story of a Jewish man who had been attacked by robbers. Luckily, a kind Samaritan happened by. And even though Jews and Samaritans were enemies, the Samaritan rescued the injured man.

And the meaning of the story is this: Jesus wants us to be kind to everyone, not just to our families and our friends. Jesus wants us to be good neighbors to all people, not just to those who are exactly like us.

Are you a good Samaritan? If so, you're doing the right thing, and that's exactly how God wants you to behave.

Believe, when you are most unhappy, that there is something for you to do in the world. So long as you can sweeten another's pain, life is not in vain.

Helen Keller

Life's most persistent and urgent question is, "What are we doing for others?"

Martin Luther King, Jr.

## TODAY'S BRIGHT IDEA

Look around: Someone very near you may need a helping hand or a kind word, so keep your eyes open, and look for people who need your help, whether at home, at church, or at school.

## PRAYER OF THE DAY

Dear Lord, make me a Good Samaritan. Let me never be too busy or too proud to help a person in need. You have given me so many blessings, Lord. Let me share those blessings with others today and every day that I live. Amen

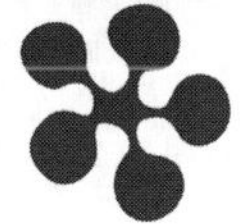

# WHEN PEOPLE ARE NOT NICE

If someone does wrong to you,
do not pay him back by doing wrong to him.

Romans 12:17 ICB

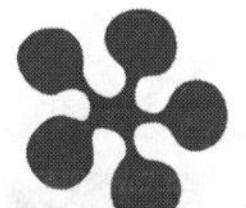

Sometimes people aren't nice, and that's when we feel like striking back in anger. But the Bible tells us not to do it. As Christians, we should not repay one bad deed with another bad deed. Instead, we should forgive the other person as quickly as we can.

Are you angry at someone? If so, then it's time to forgive him or her. Jesus does not intend that your heart be troubled by anger. Your heart should instead be filled with love, just as Jesus' heart was . . . and is!

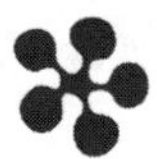

Keep away from people who try to belittle your ambitions.

Mark Twain

Misery is a communicable disease.

Martha Graham

## TODAY'S BRIGHT IDEA

Forgive . . . and keep forgiving! Sometimes, you may forgive someone once and then, at a later time, become angry at the very same person again. If so, you must forgive that person again and again . . . until it sticks!

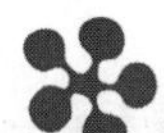

## PRAYER OF THE DAY

Dear Lord, whenever I am angry,
give me a forgiving heart.
And help me remember that
the best day to forgive
somebody is this one.
Amen

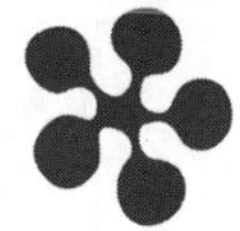

## DAY 12

# IT STARTS IN THE HEART

Blessed are the pure of heart,
for they will see God.

Matthew 5:8 NIV

Where does kindness start? It starts in our hearts and works its way out from there. Jesus taught us that a pure heart is a wonderful blessing. It's up to each of us to fill our hearts with love for God, love for Jesus, and love for all people. When we do, we are blessed.

Do you want to be the best person you can be? Then invite the love of Christ into your heart and share His love with your family and friends. And remember that lasting love always comes from a pure heart . . . like yours!

The God who dwells in heaven is willing
to dwell also in the heart of
the humble believer.

Warren Wiersbe

The health of anything—whether
a garden plant or a heart devoted to God—
reflects what is going on
(or not going on!) underground.

Elizabeth George

## TODAY'S BRIGHT IDEA

Learn about Jesus and His attitude. Then try and do what Jesus would do.

## PRAYER OF THE DAY

Dear Lord, give me a heart that is pure. Let me live by Your Word and trust in Your Son today and forever. Amen

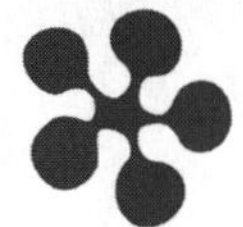

# PRAY ABOUT IT!

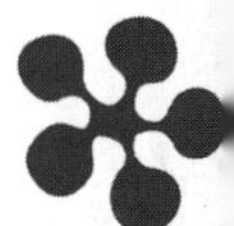

Do not worry about anything.
But pray and ask God
for everything you need.

Philippians 4:6 ICB

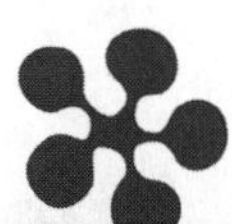

If you are upset, pray about it. If you're having trouble being kind to someone, pray about it. If there is a person you don't like, pray for a forgiving heart. If there is something you're worried about, ask God to comfort you. And as you pray more, you'll discover that God is always near and that He's always ready to hear from you. So don't worry about things; pray about them. God is waiting . . . and listening!

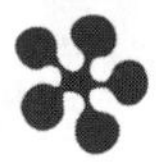

To me, faith means not worrying.

John Dewey

Worry is a poor substitute for work.

J. R. Freeman

## TODAY'S BRIGHT IDEA

Open-eyed prayers: When you are praying, your eyes don't always have to be closed. Of course it's good to close your eyes and bow your head, but you can also offer a quick prayer to God with your eyes open. That means that you can pray any time you want.

## PRAYER OF THE DAY

Dear Lord, You are always near;
let me talk with You often.
Let me use prayer to find
Your answers for my life today
and every day that I live.
Amen

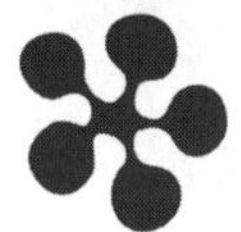

## DAY 14

# BEING HONEST AND KIND

Good people will be guided by honesty.

Proverbs 11:3 ICB

Maybe you've heard this phrase: "Honesty is the best policy." But, honesty is not just the best policy; it is also God's policy.

An important part of becoming a good person is learning to tell the truth. Lies usually have a way of hurting people, so even when it's hard, we must be honest with others.

If we are going to follow the rules that God has given us, we must remember that truth is not just the best way; it is also His way. So be honest and kind . . . now!

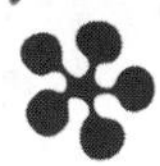

Honesty is the first chapter in
the book of wisdom.

Thomas Jefferson

How much pleasanter it would be,
and how much more would be accomplished,
if we did not give our word unless we
intended to keep it, so that we would all
know what we could depend upon.

Laura Ingalls Wilder

## TODAY'S BRIGHT IDEA

Honesty in Action: Thinking about being an honest person isn't enough. If you want to be considered an honest person, you must tell the truth today and every day.

## PRAYER OF THE DAY

Dear Lord, sometimes it's hard to tell the truth. But even when telling the truth is difficult, let me follow Your commandment. Honesty isn't just the best policy, Lord; it's Your policy, and I will obey You by making it my policy, too.

Amen

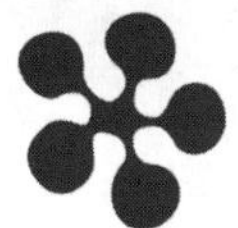

DAY 15

# MAKING FRIENDS

A friend loves you all the time.

Proverbs 17:17 ICB

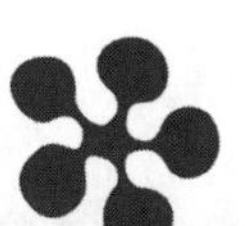

The Bible tells us that friendship can be a wonderful thing. That's why it's good to know how to make and to keep good friends.

If you want to make lots of friends, practice the Golden Rule with everybody you know. Be kind. Share. Say nice things. Be helpful. When you do, you'll discover that the Golden Rule isn't just a nice way to behave; it's also a great way to make and to keep friends!

Do you want to be wise? Choose wise friends.

Charles Swindoll

My special friends, who know me so well
and love me anyway, give me
daily encouragement to keep on.

Emilie Barnes

## TODAY'S BRIGHT IDEA

First, become interested in them . . . and soon they'll become interested in you!

## PRAYER OF THE DAY

Dear Lord, help me to be a good friend. Let me treat other people as I want to be treated. Let me share my things, and let me share kind words with my friends and family, today and every day.

Amen

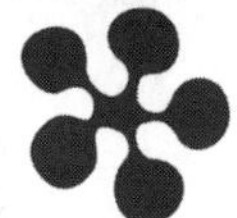

# SHARING YOUR STUFF

God loves the person who gives cheerfully.

2 Corinthians 9:7 NLT

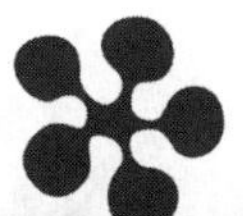

How many times have you heard someone say, "Don't touch that; it's mine!" If you're like most of us, you've heard those words many times and you may have even said them yourself.

The Bible tells us that it's better for us to share things than it is to keep them all to ourselves. And the Bible also tells us that when we share, it's best to do so cheerfully. So today and every day, let's share. It's the best way because it's God's way.

He climbs highest who helps another up.

Zig Ziglar

If we can learn to develop a giving heart toward those in our own homes and families, we'll be much more free to give ungrudgingly—and at the Spirit's prompting—to those in the most desperate need.

Mary Hunt

## TODAY'S BRIGHT IDEA

Too many toys? Give them away! Are you one of those lucky kids who has more toys than you can play with? If so, remember that not everyone is so lucky. Ask your parents to help you give some of your toys to children who need them more than you do.

## PRAYER OF THE DAY

Dear Lord, You have given me so much. Let me share my gifts with others, and let me be a joyful and generous Christian, today and every day.
Amen

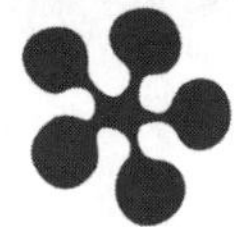

# BEING KIND TO PARENTS

Honor your father and your mother.

Exodus 20:12 ICB

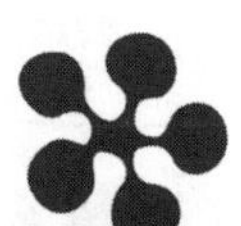

We love our parents so very much, but sometimes, we may take them for granted. When we take them "for granted," that means that we don't give them the honor and respect they deserve.

The Bible tells us to honor our parents. That's God's rule, and it's also the best way to live. When we treat our parents with the respect they deserve, we show them that we appreciate all they have done for us. And that's so much better than taking our parents for granted, and if you don't believe it, just ask them!

I grew up to always respect authority and respect those in charge.

Grant Hill

If you are willing to honor a person out of respect for God, you can be assured that God will honor you.

Beth Moore

## TODAY'S BRIGHT IDEA

Two magic words: Thank you! Your parents will never become tired of hearing those two little words. And while you're at it, try three more: "I love you!"

## PRAYER OF THE DAY

Dear Lord, make me respectful
and thankful. Let me give honor
and love to my parents,
and let my behavior be pleasing
to them . . . and to You.
Amen

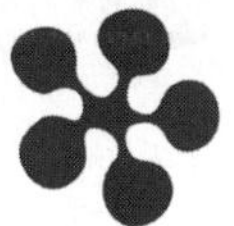

DAY 18

# SAY A KIND WORD

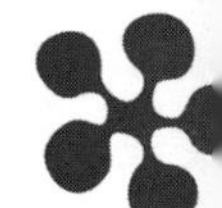

The right word spoken at the right time is as beautiful as gold apples in a silver bowl.

Proverbs 25:11 ICB

How hard is it to speak with kind words? Not very! Yet sometimes we're so busy that we forget to say the very things that might make other people feel better.

We should always try to say nice things to our families and friends. And when we feel like saying something that's not so nice, perhaps we should stop and think before we say it. Kind words help; cruel words hurt. It's as simple as that. And, when we say the right thing at the right time, we give a gift that can change someone's day or someone's life.

Kind words can be short and easy to speak,
but their echoes are truly endless.

Mother Teresa

A little kindly advice is better
than a great deal of scolding.

Fanny Crosby

## TODAY'S BRIGHT IDEA

If you don't know what to say . . . don't say anything. Sometimes, a hug works better than a whole mouthful of words.

## PRAYER OF THE DAY

Dear Lord, help me to say the right thing at the right time. Let me choose my words carefully so that I can help other people and glorify You.
Amen

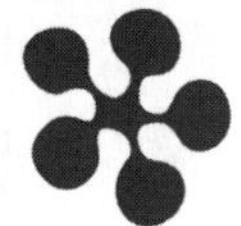

# GOD KNOWS THE HEART

I am the Lord, and I can look
into a person's heart.

Jeremiah 17:10 ICB

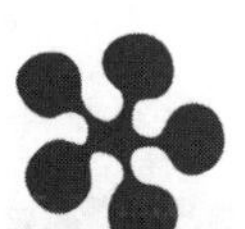

You can try to keep secrets from other people, but you can't keep secrets from God. God knows what you think and what you do. And, if you want to please God, you must start with good intentions and a kind heart.

If your heart tells you not to do something, don't do it! If your conscience tells you that something is wrong, stop! If you feel ashamed by something you've done, don't do it ever again! You can keep secrets from other people some of the time, but God is watching all of the time, and He sees everything, including your heart.

Our actions are seen by people,
but our motives are monitored by God.

Franklin Graham

God possesses infinite knowledge
and awareness which is uniquely His.
At all times, even in the midst of any type of
suffering, I can realize that He knows, loves,
watches, understands, and more than that,
He has a purpose.

Billy Graham

## TODAY'S BRIGHT IDEA

That little voice inside your head . . . is called your conscience. Listen to it; it's usually right!

## PRAYER OF THE DAY

Dear Lord, other people see me from the outside, but You know my heart. Let my heart be pure, and let me listen to the voice that You have placed there, today and always.
Amen

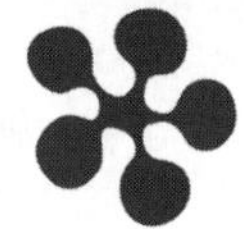

## DAY 20

# BE GENTLE

Pleasant words are like a honeycomb.
They make a person happy and healthy.

Proverbs 16:24 ICB

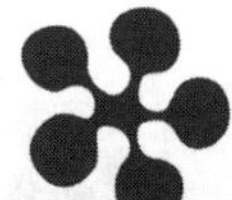

The Bible says that using gentle words is helpful and that cruel words is not. But sometimes, especially when we're frustrated or angry, our words and our actions may not be so gentle. Sometimes, we may say things or do things that are unkind or hurtful to others. When we do, we're wrong.

So the next time you're tempted to strike out in anger, don't. And if you want to help your family and friends, remember that gentle words are better than harsh words and good deeds are better than the other kind. Always!

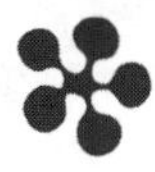

Nothing is so strong as gentleness;
nothing is so gentle as real strength.

St. Francis de Sales

If a lion's roar isn't getting you any place,
try a bear hug.

Anonymous

## TODAY'S BRIGHT IDEA

Count to ten . . . and keep counting: If you're mad at someone, don't say the first thing that comes to your mind and don't strike out in anger. Instead, catch your breath and start counting until you are once again in control of your temper. If you get to a million and you're still counting, go to bed! You'll feel better in the morning.

## PRAYER OF THE DAY

Dear Lord, help me to keep away
from angry thoughts and angry people.
And if I am tempted to have
a temper tantrum, help me to
calm down before I do.
Amen

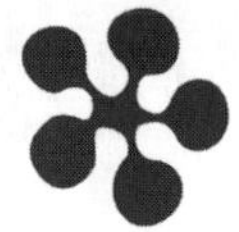

## DAY 21

# TELLING TALES

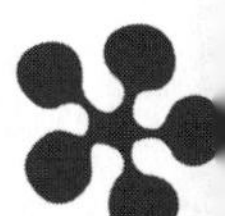

A person who gossips ruins friendships.

Proverbs 16:28 ICB

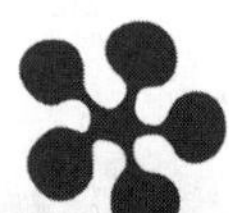

Do you know what gossip is? It's when we say bad things about people who are not around. When we gossip, we hurt others and we hurt ourselves. That's why the Bible tells us that gossip is wrong.

Sometimes, it's tempting to say bad things about people, and when we do, it makes us feel important . . . for a while. But, after a while, the bad things that we say come back to hurt us, and, of course, they hurt other people, too.

So if you want to be a kind person and a good friend, don't gossip . . . and don't listen to people who do.

You can tell more about a person
by what he says about others than
you can by what others say about him.

Leo Aikman

All cruelty springs from weakness.

Seneca

## TODAY'S BRIGHT IDEA

Watch what you say: Don't say something behind someone's back that you wouldn't say to that person directly.

## PRAYER OF THE DAY

Dear Lord, I know that I have influence on many people . . . make me an influence for good. And let the words that I speak today be worthy of the One who has saved me forever.

Amen

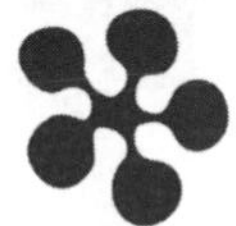

# BE KIND TO EVERYONE

Show respect for all people. Love the brothers and sisters of God's family.

1 Peter 2:17 ICB

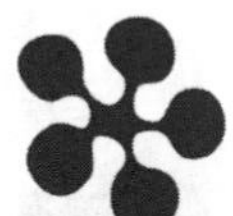

Who deserves our respect? Grown-ups? Of course. Teachers? Certainly. Family members? Yes. Friends? That's right, but it doesn't stop there. The Bible teaches us to treat all people with respect.

Respect for others is habit-forming: the more we do it, the easier it becomes. So start practicing right now. Say lots of kind words and do lots of kind things, because when it comes to kindness and respect, practice makes perfect.

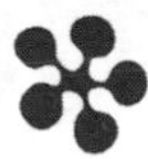

It is my calling to treat every human being
with grace and dignity, to treat every person,
whether encountered in a palace
or a gas station, as a life made
in the image of God.

Sheila Walsh

What is your focus today?
Joy comes when it is Jesus first,
others second...then you.

Kay Arthur

## TODAY'S BRIGHT IDEA

Respecting all kinds of people: Make sure that you show proper respect for everyone, even if that person happens to be different from you. It's easy to make fun of people who seem different . . . but it's wrong.

## PRAYER OF THE DAY

Dear Lord, help me to be kind to everyone I meet. Help me to be respectful to all people, not just teachers and parents. Help me to say kind words and do good deeds, today and every day.

Amen

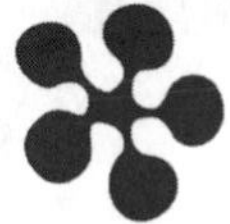

DAY 23

# PAUL AND HIS FRIENDS

I thank my God every time I remember you.

Philippians 1:3 NIV

In his letter to the Philippians, Paul wrote to his distant friends saying that he thanked God every time He remembered them. We, too, should thank God for the family and friends He has brought into our lives.

Today, let's give thanks to God for all the people who love us, for brothers and sisters, parents and grandparents, aunts and uncles, cousins, and friends. And then, as a way of thanking God, let's obey Him by being especially kind to our loved ones. They deserve it, and so does He.

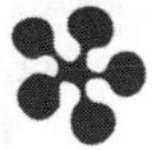

Sometimes our light goes out but is blown into flame by another human being. Each of us owes deepest thanks to those who have rekindled this light.

Albert Schweitzer

When children become adults, they remember the little things you did together, like playing ball, roasting marshmallows, or hiking a trail. They rarely remember toys.

Barbara Johnson

## TODAY'S BRIGHT IDEA

The mailman can help: If you have friends or relatives who are far away, send them letters or drawings (your mom or dad will be happy to mail them for you). Everybody loves to receive mail, and so will your family members and friends.

## PRAYER OF THE DAY

Dear Lord, thank You for my family and my friends. Let me show kindness to all of them: those who are here at home and those who are far away. Then, my family and friends will know that I remember them and love them, today and every day.

Amen

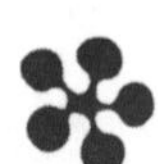

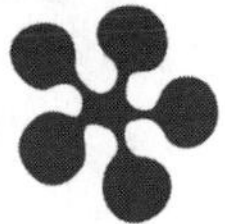

## DAY 24

# WHEN YOU'RE ANGRY

A foolish person loses his temper.
But a wise person controls his anger.

Proverbs 29:11 ICB

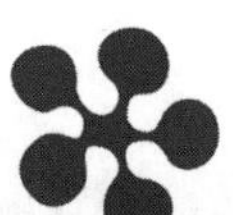

Temper tantrums are so silly. And so is pouting. So, of course, is whining. When we lose our tempers, we say things that we shouldn't say, and we do things that we shouldn't do. Too bad!

The Bible tells us that it is foolish to become angry and that it is wise to remain calm. That's why we should learn to control our tempers before our tempers control us.

Why lose your temper if, by doing so,
you offend God, annoy other people,
give yourself a bad time . . . and, in the end,
have to find it again?

Josemaria Escriva

The worst-tempered people I've ever met
were people who knew they were wrong.

Wilson Mizner

## TODAY'S BRIGHT IDEA

No more temper tantrums! If you think you're about to throw a tantrum, slow down, catch your breath, and walk away if you must. It's better to walk away than it is to strike out in anger.

## PRAYER OF THE DAY

Dear Lord, I can be so impatient,
and I can become so angry.
Calm me down, Lord, and make me
a patient, forgiving Christian.
Just as You have forgiven me,
let me forgive others so that I can
follow the example of Your Son.
Amen

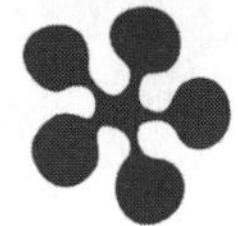

# WHEN PEOPLE CAN'T HELP THEMSELVES

I tell you the truth, whatever you did for one of the least of these brothers of mine, you did for me.

Matthew 25:40 NIV

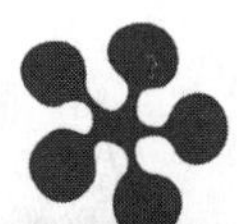

Perhaps you have lots of advantages. Some people don't. Perhaps you have the benefit of a loving family, a strong faith in God, and three good meals each day. Some people don't. Perhaps you were lucky enough to be born into a country where people are free. Some people weren't.

Jesus instructed us to care for those who can't care for themselves, wherever they may be. And, when we do something nice for someone in need, we have also done a good deed for our Savior. So today, look for someone who needs your help, and then do your best to help him or her. God is watching and waiting. The next move is yours.

Reach out and care for someone who needs the touch of hospitality. The time you spend caring today will be a love gift that will blossom into the fresh joy of God's Spirit in the future.

Emilie Barnes

Before you can dry another's tears, you too must weep.

Barbara Johnson

## TODAY'S BRIGHT IDEA

When am I old enough to start giving? If you're old enough to understand these words, you're old enough to start giving to your church and to those who are less fortunate than you. If you're not sure about the best way to do it, ask your parents!

## PRAYER OF THE DAY

Dear Lord, You have given me so many blessings. Make me a cheerful, generous giver, Lord, as I share the blessings that You first shared with me.
Amen

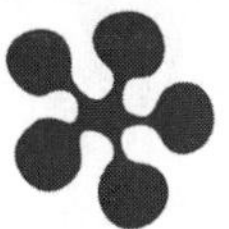

# HOW TO BE HAPPY

Those who want to do right more than anything else are happy.

Matthew 5:6 ICB

Do you want to be happy? Here are some things you should do: Love God and His Son, Jesus; obey the Golden Rule; and always try to do the right thing. When you do these things, you'll discover that happiness goes hand-in-hand with good behavior.

The happiest people do not misbehave; the happiest people are not cruel or greedy. The happiest people don't say unkind things. The happiest people are those who love God and follow His rules—starting, of course, with the Golden one.

I love my work, but work itself doesn't
add up to happiness.
Happiness is sharing another life.

Michael Landon

Joy is not in things, it is in us.

Richard Wagner

## TODAY'S BRIGHT IDEA

Sometimes happy, sometimes not: Even if you're a very good person, you shouldn't expect to be happy all the time. Sometimes, things will happen to make you sad, and it's okay to be sad when bad things happen to you or to your friends and family. But remember: through good times and bad, God is always with you, and you are always protected.

## PRAYER OF THE DAY

Dear Lord, make me the kind of Christian who earns happiness by doing the right thing. When I obey Your rules, Father, I will find the joy that You have in store for me. Let me find Your joy, Lord, today and always. Amen

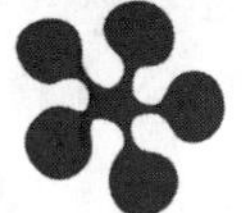

## DAY 27

# WHAT JAMES SAID

This royal law is found in the Scriptures:
"Love your neighbor as yourself."
If you obey this law, then you are doing right.

James 2:8 ICB

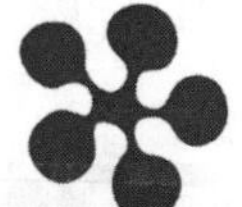

James was the brother of Jesus and a leader of the early Christian church. In a letter that is now a part of the New Testament, James reminded his friends of a "royal law." That law is the Golden Rule.

When we treat others in the same way that we wish to be treated, we are doing the right thing. James knew it and so, of course, did his brother Jesus. Now we should learn the same lesson: it's nice to be nice; it's good to be good; and it's great to be kind.

Be enthusiastic.
Every occasion is an opportunity to do good.

Russell Conwell

Seek to do good, and you will find
that happiness will run after you.

James Freeman Clarke

## TODAY'S BRIGHT IDEA

Kind is as kind does: In order to be a kind person, you must do kind things. Thinking about them isn't enough. So get busy! Your family and friends need all the kindness they can get!

## PRAYER OF THE DAY

Dear Lord, it's easy to be kind to some people and difficult to be kind to others. Let me be kind to all people so that I might follow in the footsteps of Your Son.
Amen

DAY 28

# DOING WHAT'S RIGHT

Doing what is right brings freedom
to honest people.

Proverbs 11:6 ICB

Sometimes, it's so much easier to do the wrong thing than it is to do the right thing, especially when we're tired or frustrated. But, doing the wrong thing almost always leads to trouble. And sometimes, it leads to BIG trouble.

When you do the right thing, you don't have to worry about what you did or what you said. But, when you do the wrong thing, you'll be worried that someone will find out. So do the right thing, which, by the way, also happens to be the kind thing. You'll be glad you did, and so will other people!

Life is a series of choices between
the bad, the good, and the best.
Everything depends on how we choose.

Vance Havner

The time is always right to do what is right.

Martin Luther King, Jr.

## TODAY'S BRIGHT IDEA

Think ahead: Before you do something, ask yourself this question: "Will I be ashamed if my parents find out?" If the answer to that question is "Yes," don't do it!

## PRAYER OF THE DAY

Dear Lord, I want to be a person who respects others, and I want to be a person who is kind. Wherever I am and whatever I do, let me be like Jesus in the way that I treat others, because with Him as my guide, I will do the right thing, today and forever.
Amen

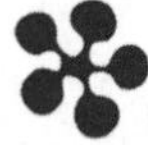

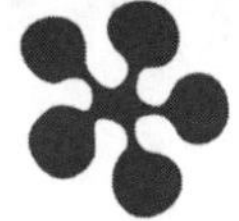

## DAY 29

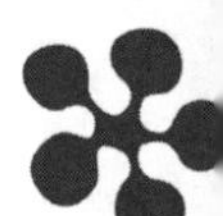

# LOVE YOUR ENEMIES

I tell you, love your enemies. Pray for those who hurt you. If you do this, you will be true sons of your Father in heaven.

Matthew 6:44-45 ICB

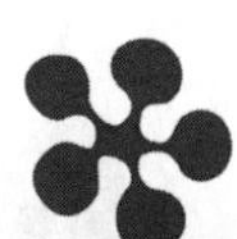

It's easy to love people who have been nice to you, but it's very hard to love people who have treated you badly. Still, Jesus instructs us to treat both our friends and our enemies with kindness and respect.

Are you having problems being nice to someone? Is there someone you know whom you don't like very much? Remember that Jesus not only forgave His enemies, He also loved them . . . and so should you.

Love your enemies,
for they tell you your faults.

Ben Franklin

I will destroy my enemies by converting
them to friends.

Maimonides

## TODAY'S BRIGHT IDEA

Making up may not be as hard as you think! If there is someone who has been mean to you, perhaps it's time for the two of you to make up. If you're willing to be the first person to offer a kind word, you'll discover that making up is usually easier than you think.

## PRAYER OF THE DAY

Dear Lord, give me a forgiving heart.
When I have bad feelings toward
another person, help me to forgive
them and to love them, just as
You forgive and love me.
Amen

# GOD IS LOVE

Whoever does not love does not know God,
because God is love.

1 John 4:8 ICB

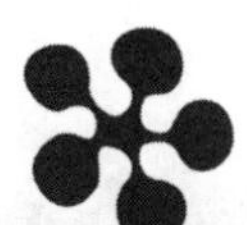

The Bible tells us that God is love and that if we wish to know Him, we must have love in our hearts. Sometimes, of course, when we're tired, frustrated, or angry, it is very hard for us to be loving. Thankfully, anger and frustration are feelings that come and go, but God's love lasts forever.

If you'd like to improve your day and your life, share God's love with your family and friends. Every time you love, every time you are kind, and every time you give, God smiles.

There's nothing you can do to get Him
to love you and there's nothing you
can do to make Him stop.

Charles Stanley

If God had a refrigerator, your picture
would be on it. If he had a wallet, your photo
would be in it. He sends you flowers
every spring and a sunrise every morning.

Max Lucado

## TODAY'S BRIGHT IDEA

Show and Tell: It's good to tell your loved ones how you feel about them, but that's not enough. You should also show them how you feel with your good deeds and your kind words.

## PRAYER OF THE DAY

Dear Lord, make me a person who is loving and giving. You first loved me, Father. Let me, in turn, love others, and let my behavior show them that I love them, today and forever.
Amen

# BIBLE VERSES TO MEMORIZE

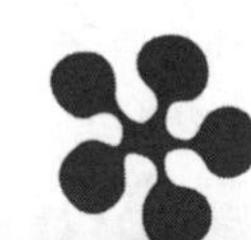

# Love is patient; love is kind.

1 Corinthians 13:4 HCSB

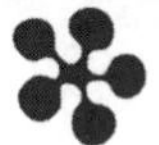

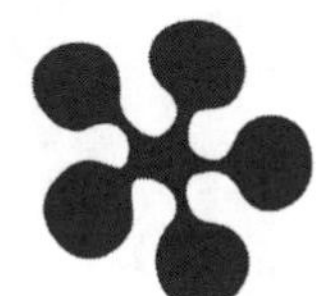

Honor your father and your mother.

Exodus 20:12 ICB

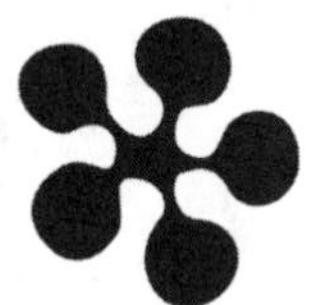

God has chosen you and made you
his holy people. He loves you.
So always do these things:
Show mercy to others, be kind,
humble, gentle, and patient.

Colossians 3:12 NCV

God loves the person who gives cheerfully.

2 Corinthians 9:7 NLT

I am not alone,
because the Father
is with Me.

John 16:32 HCSB

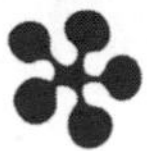

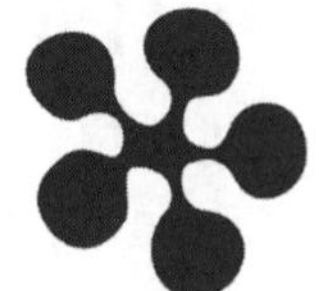

A cheerful heart is good medicine.

Proverbs 17:22 NIV

# A friend loves you all the time.

Proverbs 17:17 ICB

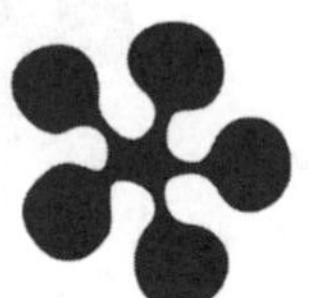

For God so loved the world
that he gave his one and only Son,
that whoever believes in him shall not
perish but have eternal life.

John 3:16 NIV

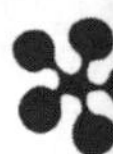

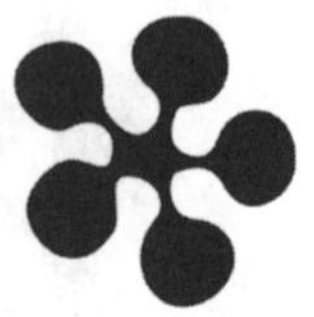

Do not worry about anything.
But pray and ask God
for everything you need.

Philippians 4:6 ICB

For to me to live is
Christ,
and to die is gain.

Philippians 1:21 KJV

# The Lord is the strength of my life.

Psalm 27:1 KJV

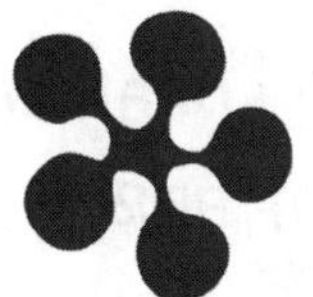

If someone does wrong to you,
do not pay him back
by doing wrong to him.

Romans 12:17 ICB

If I speak the languages of men
and of angels, but do not have love,
I am a sounding gong
or a clanging cymbal.

1 Corinthians 13:1 HCSB

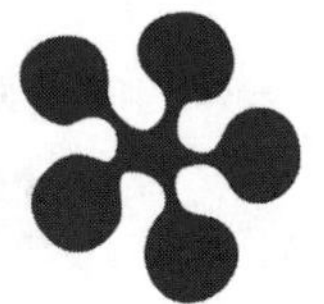

Love other people just as Christ loved us.

Ephesians 5:2 ICB

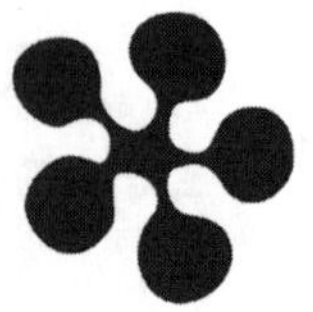

Now these three remain:
faith, hope, and love.
But the greatest of these is love.

1 Corinthians 13:13 HCSB

Do for other people
the same things you want
them to do for you.

Matthew 7:12 ICB

We must not become tired of
doing good. We will receive our harvest
of eternal life at the right time.
We must not give up!

Galatians 6:9 ICB

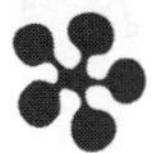

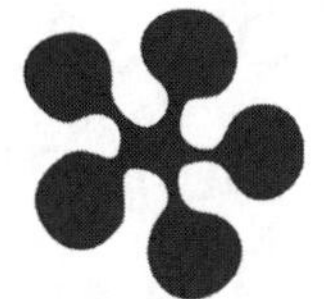

Blessed is he
that trusts
in the Lord.

Proverbs 16:20 NIV

You shall not steal,
nor deal falsely,
nor lie to one another.

Leviticus 19:11 NASB

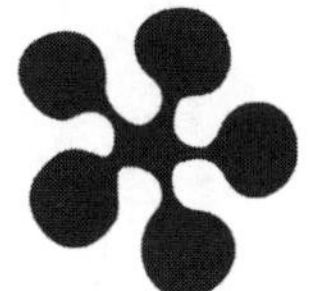

I have given you
an example to follow.
Do as I have done to you.

John 13:15 NLT

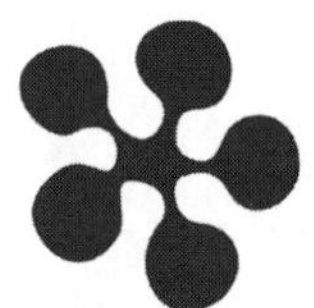

Don't ever stop being kind
and truthful.
Let kindness and truth
show in all you do.

Proverbs 3:3 ICB

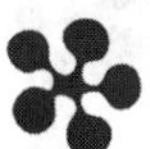

Lead a quiet
and peaceable life
in all godliness and
honesty.

1 Timothy 2:2 KJV

This, then, is how you should pray: "Our Father in heaven, hallowed be your name, your kingdom come, your will be done on earth as it is in heaven. Give us today our daily bread. Forgive us our debts, as we also have forgiven our debtors. And lead us not into temptation, but deliver us from the evil one."

Matthew 6:9-13 NIV